I read this book
all by myself

....

....

For my Uncle Joe, who keeps the
bad bugs away from *my* computer!

DON'T LET THE BAD BUGS BITE!
A Red Fox Book: 0 09 943417 2

First published in Great Britain by Red Fox in 2002
an imprint of Random House Children's Books

1 3 5 7 9 10 8 6 4 2

Text and illustrations copyright © Lindsey Gardiner 2002

Set in Cheltenham Book Infant

Red Fox Books are published by Random House Children's Books,
61–63 Uxbridge Road, London W5 5SA,
a division of The Random House Group Ltd,
in Australia by Random House Australia (Pty) Ltd,
20 Alfred Street, Milsons Point, Sydney, NSW 2061, Australia,
in New Zealand by Random House New Zealand Ltd,
18 Poland Road, Glenfield, Auckland 10, New Zealand,
and in South Africa by Random House (Pty) Ltd,
Endulini, 5A Jubilee Road, Parktown 2193, South Africa

THE RANDOM HOUSE GROUP Limited Reg. No. 954009
www.kidsatrandomhouse.co.uk

A CIP catalogue record for this book is available from the British Library.

Printed and bound in Singapore by Tien Wah Press

Don't Let the Bad Bugs Bite!

Lindsey Gardiner

RED FOX

This is Mouse.  He helps everyone do whatever they want on the computer.

Lily moves Mouse in her hand to make the cursor move on the screen. The cursor sometimes looks like an arrow.

And these are Mouse's friends:

Mum . . .

Dad . . .

. . . and Lily!

Mouse and Lily are making a special
picture for Lily's friend in America.

"Let's ask Dad to help us send our picture by e-mail," said Lily.

My mum and dad

This is Barney.

I ♥ football!

Scruffy

My Pets

	NAME	AGE	COLOUR	LIKES	DOESN'T LIKE
DOG	Barney	8	cream	biscuits	Billy
FISH	Gums	4 months	orange	swimming	Billy
BUDGIE	Billy	$3\frac{1}{2}$	blue	barking	being a budgie
GUINEA PIG	Scruffy	$1\frac{3}{4}$	brown + black	carrots	Billy

My Family

	HAIR	AGE
MUM	orange	$31\frac{1}{2}$
DAD	brown	35
GRAN	purple	58
GRANDAD	black	59

Gums the fish

Mum's car

Billy (he barks!)

Spaghetti is my favourite food.

"Time for tea, Lily!"

"Oh, no! Mum is calling me for tea," said Lily. "We'll have to send our picture later. Bye!"

CLICK.

Lily turned off the computer. ZAP! Her picture disappeared off the computer screen. Mouse blinked. Where had it gone? "Lily? Hey, Lily, wait!" he called. "Our picture is gone! I think you clicked the wrong button by mistake. LILY, COME BACK!" But Lily was gone.

Letters

Charts

Photos

Notebook

Printer

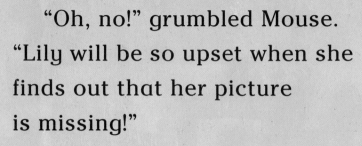

"Oh, no!" grumbled Mouse. "Lily will be so upset when she finds out that her picture is missing!"

He looked up and saw his friend Cursor sitting in the corner. "Hi, Mouse, what's up?" she asked.

"I've lost Lily's picture. It's really important," said Mouse. "Have you seen it?"

No, sorry!

Find out about Cursor and other computer words in the glossary at the back of the book.

"No, sorry," said Cursor. "But if it's that important, the bug that was here before might find it first . . ."

Music

Lily's Work

Games

E-mail

Paint Box

Saved Work

Oh, no!

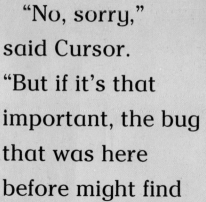

Tools

Letters

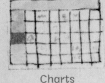

Charts

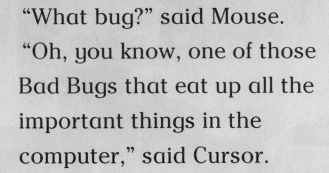

"What bug?" said Mouse.
"Oh, you know, one of those
Bad Bugs that eat up all the
important things in the
computer," said Cursor.

"You saw one of
those?" cried Mouse,
getting himself
into a tiz.

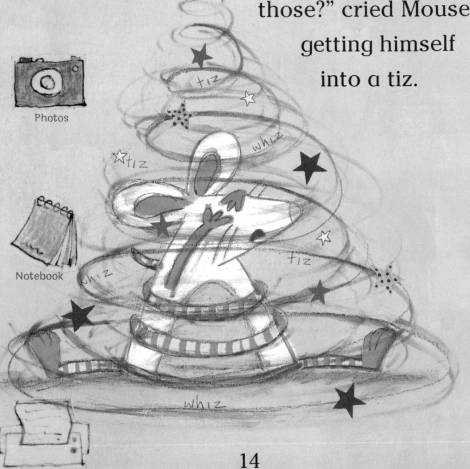

Photos

Notebook

Printer

"I'm not sure what that bug's been eating," said Cursor, "but he has bad teeth and *really* bad breath!"

Music

Lily's Work

"Yes, that type of bug is really bad . . ." said Mouse.

Games

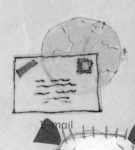
E-mail

"... and he's

really

close!"

said Cursor.

Paint Box

Clock

15

Recycle Bin

Tools

"Look! There he is, with his bad teeth and bad breath!" yelled Cursor.

"Shhh, not so loud, Cursor!" said Mouse.

"I have to find Lily's picture before the Bad Bug does. You hide and I'll go and see if the letters can help."

Mouse _____ crept

quietly   across   the   screen.

HEY, MOUSE!

"What are you in such a hurry for?" shouted the Bad Bug. "N-n-nothing!" said Mouse.

18

"I'm HUNGRY!" boomed the Bad Bug.
"I need something important to eat!"
   "H-h-here, you can have some
of my ch-ch-cheese," said Mouse.
"That always stops my
tummy rumbling."

   And before Bad Bug could
answer, Mouse scuttled off
to Letter School.

19

"Has anyone seen Lily's special picture?"
Mouse asked the letters. "There's a
Bad Bug after it!"

"No," said Lazy, yawning.

"Not us," said wiggly.

"Who cares!" said

Wicked

and

Horrible.

"Have you asked the bad words?" said SMARTYPANTS. "I bet they know something about Lily's picture."

Rumble!

Rumble!

horrid
yuck
HORRIBLE
terror
badness
horror
WICKED drea
BAD

"Yeah, I hear rumbling coming from their side," said CLEVERCLOGS.

"And I smell something rotten!" said NOSEY.

"Look, **BAD**'s hiding something, Mouse," said good.

All the letters looked at where good was pointing.

Suddenly, the Bad Bug couldn't keep quiet any longer. He jumped out with a loud rumble.

Rumble!

Rumble!

grr

Where's that picture? I'M STARVING!

"Time to go!" squeaked Mouse.
He threw some more cheese to
the Bad Bug and scuttled off to
the Picture Playground as
fast as he could go.

Bye!

"Phew! Good job I can run fast," puffed Mouse.

"Has anyone seen Lily's special picture?" he asked the pictures. "There's a bug on the loose and . . ."

swish...

swish

wag
wag

Bbbzzzzzzz

Bbbzzzzzzzzzz

All the pictures hid. "Don't worry!" cried Mouse. "It's Lily's picture he's after, not you!

"If the Bad Bug was hiding here, you would know.

Whoosh

yap yap

Help!

BUZZ BUZZ

"He's big and ugly,
with bad teeth, bad hair,
bad breath, and a really
bad temper, and . . .

Rumble!
Rumble!

"... and, oh no, I think he's following me!" cried Mouse.

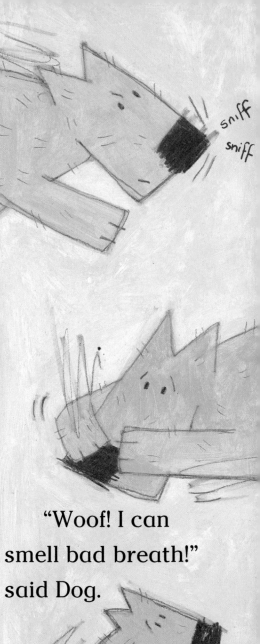

sniff
sniff

"Woof! I can smell bad breath!" said Dog.

Pooh!

"I can hear him,"
said Cat.

honk honk

"He's hiding here
somewhere,"
said Car.

"I see you . . ."
trumpeted Elephant.

"... I found you!"

Rumble!

Rumble!

"I'M STARVING,"
boomed the Bad Bug.
"MOUSE, GIVE ME THAT
PICTURE, OR ..."

"Quick, Elephant, give him this
cheese!" cried Mouse, and he scuttled off
to Number Land as fast as he could go.

"Numbers, you've got to help me find Lily's picture! It's really important to her!" puffed Mouse.

"Yes, we know," said Four.

$$2 + 2 = 4$$

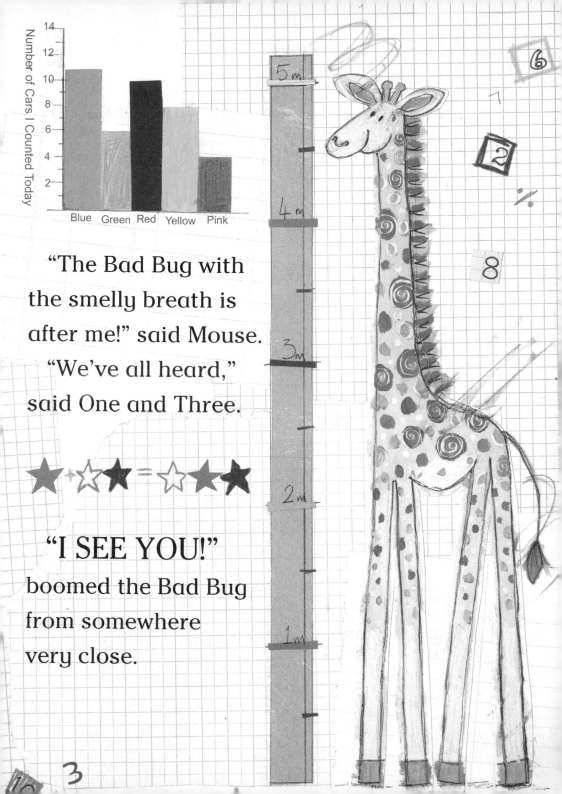

"The Bad Bug with the smelly breath is after me!" said Mouse. "We've all heard," said One and Three.

"I SEE YOU!" boomed the Bad Bug from somewhere very close.

300

Hurry, he's coming!

9 "Quick! Make a wall!" shouted Three Hundred.

"LET ME THROUGH! I'm hungry for important things!" boomed the Bad Bug.

Number Nursery

go, Mouse!

1 2 3 4 5 6 7 8 9 10 11 12

1 + 1 = 2

Good luck

RUN RUN !

6 + 2 = 8

"Run, Mouse, run!" called the numbers. "Quickly, before he gets through our wall!"

"That cheese doesn't fill me up!" boomed the Bad Bug, coming closer.

Mouse ran.

He ran and ran, all the way back to the main screen.

"Help, Cursor!" he puffed. "The Bad Bug is after me!"

Music

Lily's Work

Games

E-mail

Paint Box

Saved Work

Clock

Tools

"Jump in the recycle bin!" said Cursor. "That fat bug will never fit in there!"

Recycle Bin

Mouse jumped in and landed on something familiar. "Hey, I've found Lily's picture!" he squeaked.

The Bad Bug stuck his head inside the bin.

He tried to steal the picture.

GIVE ME THAT! I'm starving!

he boomed.

Mouse grabbed the
picture back. "Sorry,
I have to run," he said.
   He hopped back out
of the bin and
slammed on the
lid tight.

39

CLICK! Mouse emptied the recycle bin.

"Phew! That was close," he puffed. "Now all the rubbish and the Bad Bug have disappeared for ever!

"And just in time for me to put the picture back because . . .

41

"... here comes Lily!"

My mum and dad

This is Barney.

I ♥ football!

Scruffy

My Pets

	HAIR	AGE	COLOUR	LIKES	DOESN'T LIKE
DOG	Barney	8	cream	biscuits	Billy
FISH	Gums	4 months	orange	swimming	Billy
BUDGIE	Billy	$3\frac{1}{2}$	blue	barking	being a budgie
GUINEA PIG	Scruffy	$1\frac{3}{4}$	brown + black	carrots	Billy

My Family

	HAIR	AGE
MUM	orange	$31\frac{1}{2}$
DAD	brown	35
GRAN	purple	58
GRANDAD	black	59

Gums the fish

Mum's car

Billy (he barks!)

baghetti is my favourite food.

Cheese!

Use a computer to make a picture like Lily's. Ask an adult to help get you started.

You can draw pictures on your computer in the picture program. Use your mouse as a pencil or a paint brush.

Scan in a photograph of a friend or pet.

Lily's Room
PLEASE KNOCK
Before you enter!

Use different fonts to make a sign.

MAKE A FACE using the letters 'W', 'I' and 'O':

o o
I
WWWW

Draw a circle round them.

Use different shapes to make a picture. Try colouring them in.

I'm made with circles.

Glossary

Computer Bug: I am also called a virus. I attack important files on your computer.

Cursor: sometimes I appear as an arrow, sometimes as a flashing line. Click on me with your mouse, and you can type in words or numbers where I am.

Icons: we are the small pictures you see on the computer screen. You double-click on us to get into a program.

Mouse: you move me with your hand to click on the screen and to move the cursor around. If you double-click on me, I open things.

Program: I help your computer to answer questions, get information, or solve problems. For example, you use a word program to write a letter or a games program to play a game.

Recycle bin: your rubbish stays here until you empty me. Then it is rubbed out of the computer's memory for ever.

Screen

Keyboard

Mouse

45

Me in the studio

Meet the author.

Lindsey Gardiner

What did you use to paint the pictures in this book? EVERYTHING! I used paint, pencils, pastels, ink and collage. (And even the computer in some bits!)

How long did it take to do the pictures? It took me a few months to write this story and a few months to do all the artwork. (Doing the artwork is always more fun for me!)

Do you use the computer to make pictures like Lily does? Sometimes, but I prefer to use pencils. I use the computer to print things out in different colours and patterns. Then I chop them up and use them for collage on top of my paint.

Do you use the computer to e-mail friends who are far away? Yes, all the time! It's great. You can send pictures, cards and photos to them and they get them right away.

What's your favourite place to draw? I have a studio, which I share with my dog Lola. I don't have to tidy up very often. (Until Lola starts eating up bits of collage off the floor that is!)

Me and Lola

Did you draw when you were a child?
Yes, all the time. I had to have my felt-tip pens taken away from me when I went to bed at night! All I ever wanted to be was an artist – and here I am!

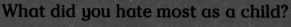
Lola panting

What did you hate most as a child?
I've ALWAYS hated having to go to bed, especially in the summer. I think there should be a few extra hours in every day so I can fit everything in!

What do you do if you get stuck on a drawing? I don't really get stuck on drawing, but I do get stuck on writing! Then it's best to go and do something else altogether and not worry about it. I usually become unstuck in the middle of the night and have to scribble things down. (I keep a notebook under my pillow.)

Can I be an illustrator like you? Yes, as long as you love drawing! It's great fun. I couldn't think of anything better than getting to draw and paint every day.

Will you write or draw a story too?

Let your ideas take flight with
Flying Foxes

Slow Magic
by Pippa Goodhart and John Kelly

Magic Mr Edison
by Andrew Melrose and Katja Bandlow

Only Tadpoles Have Tails
by Jane Clarke and Jane Gray

That's Not Right!
by Alan Durant and Katharine McEwen

Don't Let the Bad Bugs Bite!
by Lindsey Gardiner

A Tale of Two Wolves
by Susan Kelly and Lizzie Finlay

All the Little Ones – and a Half
by Mary Murphy

Sherman Swaps Shells
by Jane Clarke and Ant Parker

Digging for Dinosaurs
by Judy Waite and Garry Parsons

Shadowhog
by Sandra Ann Horn and Mary McQuillan

The Magic Backpack
by Julia Jarman and Adriano Gon

Jake and the Red Bird
by Ragnhild Scamell and Valeria Petrone